FOR THE BRIDE AND GROOM

Very best wishes to a
super sis- Love
BOOP

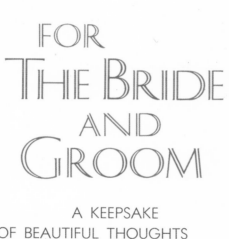

FOR THE BRIDE AND GROOM

A KEEPSAKE
OF BEAUTIFUL THOUGHTS
ON LOVE AND MARRIAGE

♛ Hallmark Editions

Editorial Research: Tina Hacker
Editorial Direction: Aileene Neighbors

The publisher wishes to thank those who have given their kind permission to reprint material included in this book. Every effort has been made to give proper acknowledgments. Any omissions or errors are deeply regretted, and the publisher, upon notification, will be pleased to make necessary corrections in subsequent editions.

Acknowledgments: "Love" from The Gypsy Heart by Emily Carey Alleman. Copyright 1957 by Emily Carey Alleman. Used by permission of the author. Genesis 2:24 from the King James Version Bible. Reprinted by permission of the Cambridge University Press. Published by the Syndics of Cambridge University Press. "Afterwards" from The Heart of Home by Anne Campbell. Used by permission of the author. "The Best Day to Wed," "When to Marry," "Bridal Colors," "June Wedding," and "The Wedding Ring" from The Folklore of Weddings and Marriage, edited by Duncan Emrich. Reprinted by permission of John Cushman Associates, Inc. Copyright © 1970 by Duncan Emrich. "Most Remembered" by Katherine Edelman. Reprinted by permission of The Kansas City Star. Excerpt from Marriage & Morals by Bertrand Russell. Copyright 1929, renewed 1957 by Bertrand Russell. Reprinted by permission of the publishers, Horace Liveright, Inc. and George Allen & Unwin Ltd. Excerpt from Love by Walter de la Mare. Copyright 1946 by Walter de la Mare. Reprinted by permission of The Literary Trustees of Walter de la Mare, and The Society of Authors as their representative.

FOR THE BRIDE AND GROOM

Your wedding — what occasion could ever be more exciting to anticipate or more wonderful to recall? This is truly a time of incomparable delight, the beginning of a whole new lifetime of dreams and blessings to share, the beautiful celebration of your true and lasting devotion.

Gathered in this keepsake edition are many unforgettable poems, verses, quotations and reflections on love and marriage. Here are words of warmth and feeling to commemorate the gladness of your special day, words of wisdom and inspiration you will cherish through all the years ahead.

May you find this richly illustrated collection a lovely way to remember the joys of this special time in your lives. And may it help convey the promise of even greater happiness for you as husband and wife. Congratulations to both of you — and best wishes for today, tomorrow and always.

JOINING TWO LIVES TOGETHER

A bride in white
   walking down the aisle,
A bridegroom waiting with a smile,
A spoken vow, a pledge to love,
A prayer for blessings
   from above,
Wedding bands
   slipped into place,
A tender kiss and warm embrace;
What a wonderful day
   in your life —
The day you become
   "man and wife"!

Kay Andrew

Some things are forever new —
      first love's halting phrases...
   the magic of discovery...
         the sudden singing
                of the heart.

H. Perry

Those who have never known the deep intimacy
      and the intense companionship of happy mutual love
  have missed the best thing
      that life has to give....

Bertrand Russell

THIS IS MARRIAGE

This is marriage...
      The blending of two happy hearts
        who share a dream come true,
      A dream that's filled with hope and joy
        to last a lifetime through.

      The union of two thankful hearts
        who find that life can hold
      A treasure of true happiness
        that's worth far more than gold.

      The triumph of two loving hearts
        who know the glory of
      The greatest blessing life can bring —
        the miracle of love.
      ...This is marriage.

Edward Cunningham

TO A FLOWER GIRL

You are a flower, littlest one, as pink
As any in your miniature bouquet,
Or pinker. And it's you, small friend, I think
The bride's depending on. You lead the way
With slow and careful step. But, oh, your eyes
Are tattletales! No moment's glad surprise
Will catch you unaware. You bless the aisle
You walk upon....

                    And suddenly your smile
(A jack-o'-lantern's own, but twice as wide)
Lights up your face — and ours. Here comes
        the bride,
And you've just learned what there is no forgetting,
From six to sixty, women *love* a wedding!

Maureen Cannon

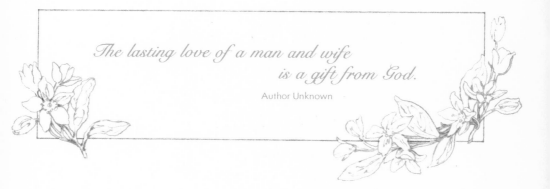

*The lasting love of a man and wife
                is a gift from God.*

Author Unknown

TRUE LOVE

My true-love hath my heart, and I have his,
By just exchange one for another given:
I hold his dear, and mine he cannot miss,
There never was a better bargain driven:
My true-love hath my heart, and I have his.

His heart in me keeps him and me in one,
My heart in him his thoughts and sense guides:
He loves my heart, for once it was his own,
I cherish his because in me it bides:
My true-love hath my heart, and I have his.

Sir Philip Sidney

Time is
    Too slow for those who wait,
      Too swift for those who fear,
    Too long for those who grieve,
      Too short for those who rejoice;
  But for those who love,
    Time is not.

Henry van Dyke

TRADITION

Something Old —
    Wear something old from a bygone year
    Which, like your love, is lasting and dear.
Something New —
    Wear something new as a token, too,
    Of the wonderful life that's beginning for you.
Something Borrowed —
    Wear something borrowed and it will tell
    That friends and loved ones wish you well.
Something Blue —
    Wear something blue, like the skies above,
    When two hearts enter a world of love.
And a Penny, Too —
    And place a penny inside your shoe
    To assure good fortune your whole life through.

Anne Parker

Marriage consists
    not in two people looking into each other's eyes,
  but in two people,
    standing shoulder to shoulder,
    both looking in the same direction.

Halford E. Luccock

When the conquering Roman legions entered Portugal in the third century, a marriage was arranged between the victorious Roman general and a beautiful princess of the Portuguese royal family. He had loved her ever since he first heard stories of her beauty and charm. Although she admired him, the princess also feared him because of the stories she had heard of his fierceness in battle.

At a sumptuous banquet before the wedding, the bride and groom saw one another for the first time. But silence came between them — a silence of awe on her part and a silence of love on his. After the banquet, the general walked alone across the palace grounds to his encampment.

"How beautiful she is," he thought. "If only I could drive the fear from her eyes and let her know that I would love her tenderly all our lives."

As he walked, he found himself in a garden of small orange trees. "How fragrant they are! Like the perfume in her hair. And purest white, like her own pure soul."

Prompted by these thoughts, he gathered a spray of the lovely orange blossoms and sent them by messenger to the princess. She was so touched by this tender gift from the great soldier that she shyly joined him in the garden. Soon they were walking hand in hand among the orange blossoms, and in her heart a quiet love grew that matched his own.

On their wedding day, the princess carried a spray of orange blossoms. Since that time these white flowers, a symbol of deepest love, have been carried by brides everywhere.

Marriages are made in heaven.

Alfred, Lord Tennyson

TIMELESS MEMORIES

The wedding march, the altar's glow,
Vows repeated soft and low,
A wedding prayer, a golden band,
Happy couple hand-in-hand,
Congratulations and advice,
Fond farewells and shoes and rice,
Time of laughter, smiles and tears,
Memories for all your years.

George Dean Walley

I SEARCH FOR WORDS

I search for words to fashion into speech
The form and substance of our love; as well
Try to define a mountain's lofty reach
Or ocean's crashing sound within a shell.
One cannot capture sunlight's dappled sheen
Or the spiraling and rush of swallows wings;
And who can tell of meadows, gold and green,
Or prison earth's majestic, lovely things?
No words, however eloquent, convey
The radiance that shimmers in a star,
Nor sound the depth of beauty before day
Or tell the sweet enchantment where you are.
I search for words, but none can quite reveal
The depth and beauty of the love we feel.

Mary Dawson Hughes

A PERFECT ONE

As two rivers
    flow into one stream…
  As two visions
     blend into one dream…
  As dawn and dusk
     reveal a single sun…
From two beautiful lives…
   a perfect One.

Barbara Kunz Loots

13

THE BEGINNING OF AN IMMORTAL LOVE STORY

The love story between the poets Elizabeth Barrett and Robert Browning began with these letters.

Robert Browning to Elizabeth Barrett

New Cross, Hatcham, Surrey
January 10th, 1845

I love your verses with all my heart, dear Miss Barrett — and this is no off-hand complimentary letter that I shall write, — whatever else, no prompt matter-of-course recognition of your genius, and there a graceful and natural end of the thing. Since the day last week when I first read your poems, I quite laugh to remember how I have been turning and turning again in my mind what I should be able to tell you of their effect upon me, for in the first flush of delight I thought I would this once get out of my habit of purely passive enjoyment, when I do really enjoy, and thoroughly justify my admiration — perhaps even, as a loyal fellow-craftsman should, try and find fault and do you some little good to be proud of hereafter! — but nothing comes of it all — so into me has it gone, and part of me has it become, this great living poetry of yours, not a flower of which but took root and grew — Oh, how different that is from lying to be dried and pressed flat, and prized highly, and put in a book with a proper account at top and bottom, and shut up and put away... and the book called a "Flora," besides! After all, I need not give up the thought of doing that, too, in time; because even now, talking with whoever is worthy, I can

14

give a reason for my faith in one and another excellence, the fresh strange music, the affluent language, the exquisite pathos and true new brave thought; but in thus addressing myself to you — your own self, and for the first time, my feeling rises altogether. I do, as I say, love these books with all my heart — and I love you too. Do you know I was once not very far from seeing — really seeing you? Mr. Kenyon said to me one morning "Would you like to see Miss Barrett?," then he went to announce me, — then he returned…you were too unwell, and now it is years ago, and I feel as at some untoward passage in my travels, as if I had been close, so close, to some world's-wonder in chapel or crypt, only a screen to push and I might have entered, but there was some slight, so it now seems, slight and just sufficient bar to admission, and the half-opened door shut, and I went home my thousands of miles, and the sight was never to be?

Well, these Poems were to be, and this true thankful joy and pride with which I feel myself,

Yours ever faithfully,
Robert Browning

Elizabeth's Answer

50 Wimpole Street
January 11th, 1845

I thank you, dear Mr. Browning, from the bottom of my heart. You meant to give me pleasure by your letter — and even if the object had not been answered, I ought still to thank you. But it is thoroughly answered. Such a letter from such a hand! Sympathy is dear — very dear to me: but the sympathy of a poet, and of such a poet, is the quintessence of sympathy of me! Will you take back my gratitude for it? — agreeing, too, that of all the commerce done in the world, from Tyre to Carthage, the exchange of sympathy for gratitude is the most princely thing!

For the rest you draw me on with your kindness. It is difficult to get rid of people when you once have given them too much pleasure — *that* is a fact, and we will not stop for the moral of it. What I was going to say — after a little natural hesitation — is, that if ever you emerge without inconvenient effort from your "passive state," and will *tell* me of such faults as rise to the surface and strike you as important in my poems (for of course, I do not think of troubling you with criticism in detail), you will confer a lasting obligation on me, and one which I shall value so much, that I covet it at a distance. I do not pretend to any extraordinary meekness under criticism and it is possible enough that I might not be altogether obedient to yours. But with my high respect for your power in your Art and for your experience as an artist, it would be quite impossible for me to hear a general observation of yours on what appear to you my master-faults, without being the better for it hereafter in some way....

Is it indeed true that I was so near to the pleasure and honour of making your acquaintance and can it be true that you look back upon the lost opportunity with any regret? *But* — you know — if you had entered the "crypt," you might have caught cold, or been tired to death, and *wished* yourself "a thousand miles off"; which would have been worse than travelling them. It is not my interest, however, to put such thoughts in your head about its being "all for the best"; and I would rather hope (as I do) that what I lost by one chance I may recover by some future one....

I am writing too much, — and notwithstanding that I am writing too much, I will write of one thing more. I will say that I am your debtor, not only for this cordial letter and for all the pleasure which came with it, but in other ways, and those the highest: and I will say that while I live to follow the divine art of poetry, in proportion to my love for it and my devotion to it, I must be a devout admirer and student of your works. This is in my heart to say to you — and I say it.

And for the rest, I am proud to remain,

Your obliged and faithful
Elizabeth B. Barrett

THE COLORS OF LOVE

New love is pink, blush.
   The whole world looks bright
When seen through
   The rose glow of delight.

Love is orange-yellow,
   Warm as the sun,
Radiant, vital,
   When two are as one.

Blue is regret
   For the words left unspoken,
Kindness forgotten,
   Promises broken.

Pure white is the love
   That comforts, that cares,
Forgetful of self,
   All burdens bears.

Gold are the memories,
   Golden the laughter,
Golden forgiveness
   And grace ever after.

Happiness, sadness,
   Peacefulness, strife —
The colors of love
   Are the colors of life.

Ruth A. Jacob

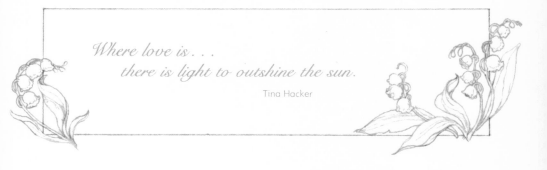

Where love is . . .
   there is light to outshine the sun.

Tina Hacker

AFTERWARDS

Afterwards it is not the kiss we remember —
   Only that one day in gold September;
Your spirit met my spirit, and we clung
   Together — wordless for one moment, hung
     In space....Afterwards recalling — not the greeting,
And not the kiss...but just our spirits meeting!

Anne Campbell

THIS HAPPY DAY

Down the aisle with radiant smile,
    Here comes the lovely bride
With her bouquet on this her day,
    Her father at her side —
Her bridal gown cascading down
    Into a flowing train,
A veil of lace about her face,
    Pearls glistening like rain —
Lovingly the groom-to-be
    Then takes her hand in his,
Their vows are said as they are wed,
    And then they gently kiss —
In every way a happy day
    With memories so sweet
That starts their life as man and wife,
    And makes their world complete.

B. Witherspoon Whitley

A GIFT FROM GOD

True love's the gift which God has given
    To man alone beneath the heaven…
It is the secret sympathy,
    The silver link, the silken tie,
Which heart to heart, and mind to mind,
    In body and in soul can bind.

Sir Walter Scott

Love is friendship set to music.

Pollock

To have and to hold from this day forward,
for better for worse,
for richer for poorer,
in sickness and in health,
to love and to cherish,
till death us do part.

Book of Common Prayer

A PARTNERSHIP

I believe that marriage should be a perfect partnership; that a woman should have all the rights that man has, and one more — the right to be protected. I do not like the man who thinks he is boss. The fellow in the dugout was always talking about being boss. I do not like a man who thinks he has got authority and that the woman belongs to him — that wants his wife for a slave. I would not want the love of a woman that is not great enough, grand enough, and splendid enough to be free. I will never give to any woman my heart upon whom I afterwards put chains.

Robert G. Ingersoll

TO BE WITH YOU

I want you near at the first break of dawn
　　When flowers are kissed by the dew.
　I need your love like the earth needs the rain,
　　Like spring needs a heaven of blue.

I want your smile when the bright noonday sun
　　Caresses your cheek and your hair
　As you walk down the rose-bordered pathway,
　　A picture of loveliness there.

I want to hear the sweet sound of your voice,
　　To be with you wherever you are
　When God gently draws the curtains of night
　　And fastens them shut with a star.

Reginald Holmes

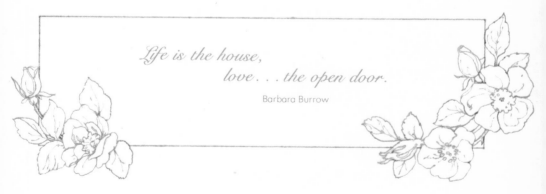

Life is the house,
　　love . . . the open door.

Barbara Burrow

23

We enter into love,
    or love enters into us,
        as purely and happily as the song of birds
            into the hush of daybreak.

Walter de la Mare

LEGEND OF THE WEDDING RING

In biblical times, a certain young king married a princess from a neighboring country. Soon after their marriage, it became necessary for the king to leave his young wife and lead his armies into battle.

One night before he left, the king was walking in the palace gardens. He stood beside the moon-drenched pool tossing pebbles into the water and watching the circles form. "How like a circle is my love for her," he thought. "It, too, has no beginning and no ending!"

The next day he called in his goldsmith and directed him to make a gold circle to fit the queen's finger. When the king slipped the finished ring on his wife's finger, he told her, "This circle, which has no beginning and no ending, is a pledge of my love for you, which is also eternal."

And down through the ages, the gold circle has sealed the vows of marriage and symbolized the purity and the endlessness of love.

NUPTIAL PRAYER

O God of wisdom, who has said
    Man should not walk alone,
Be with us now who choose to tread
    Together, as Thine own.

As we before thine altar fair
    Repeat the sacred vow,
To keep it make us now aware
    That Thou must show us how.

Be near when dark clouds roll our way
    And from temptations, free;
But when we walk through sunny days
    Make us remember Thee.

And most of all keep our faith strong,
    May it our lives enshrine,
That this love may our whole life long
    Be like to that divine.

Charlotte Carpenter

This is the true measure of love,
    when we believe that we alone can love,
    that no one could ever have loved so before us,
        and that no one will ever love
                            in the same way after us.

Johann Wolfgang von Goethe

THE BRIDESMAID

O bridesmaid, ere the happy knot was tied,
Thine eyes so wept that they could hardly see;
Thy sister smiled and said, "No tears for me!
A happy bridesmaid makes a happy bride."
And then, the couple standing side by side,
Love lighted down between them full of glee,
And over his left shoulder laugh'd at thee,
"O happy bridesmaid, make a happy bride."
And all at once a pleasant truth I learned,
For while the tender service made thee weep,
I loved thee for the tear thou couldst not hide,
And prest thy hand and knew the press returned,
And thought, "My life is sick of single sleep:
O happy bridesmaid, make a happy bride."

Alfred, Lord Tennyson

Love has the power
to alter the hour...
to shape our destiny.

George Webster Douglas

Therefore shall a man leave his father
and his mother,
and shall cleave unto his wife:
and they shall be one flesh.

Genesis 2:24

THE SHINING YEARS

These are the years: the shining years,
Young hearts' entwining years,
when two who are joined
in a world of love
find the joy
they've been dreaming of.
These are the shining years.

Shannon O'Rourke

Love is eternal…
> Like the circle of a ring,
> Whole unto itself,
> Its beauty never ending,
> But going on forever.

Katherine Nelson Davis

Two persons who love each other
> are in a place more holy
> than the interior of a church.

William Lyon Phelps

WHAT IS MARRIAGE?

Marriage is
> when two hearts know
> how wide and deep their love can grow
> as tides of living ebb and flow.

Marriage is
> when two shall be
> one, as the waters of the sea
> encircling the world--eternally.

Barbara Kunz Loots

WEDDING HYMN

Thou God, whose high, eternal Love
    Is the only blue sky of our life,
Clear all the Heaven that bends above
    The life-road of this man and wife.

May these two lives be but one note
    In the world's strange-sounding harmony,
Whose sacred music e'er shall float
    Through every discord up to Thee.

As when from separate stars two beams
    United to form one tender ray:
As when two sweet but shadowy dreams
    Explain each other in the day:

So may these two dear hearts one light
    Emit, and each interpret each.
Get an angel come and dwell to-night
    In this dear double-heart, and teach!

Sidney Lanier

To love one maiden only, cleave to her,
    and worship her by years of golden deeds.

Alfred, Lord Tennyson

HONEY-MOON

It was the custom of the higher orders of Teutones,
an ancient people who inhabited
the northern parts of Germany,
to drink mead or metheglin,
a beverage made with honey,
for thirty days after every wedding.
From this custom comes the expression
"to spend the honey-moon."

THAT FIRST DAY

I wish I could remember that first day,
First hour, first moment of your meeting me,
If bright or dim the season, it might be
Summer or Winter for aught I can say;
So unrecorded did it slip away,
So blind was I to see and to foresee,
So dull to mark the budding of my tree
That would not blossom yet for many a May.
If only I could recollect it, such
A day of days! I let it come and go
As traceless as a thaw of bygone snow;
It seemed to mean so little, meant so much;
If only now I could recall that touch,
First touch of hand in hand — did one but know!

Christina Rossetti

from THE BELLS

Hear the mellow wedding bells —
   Golden bells!
What a world of happiness their harmony foretells!
   Through the balmy air of night
How they ring out their delight! —
From the molten-golden notes,
   And all in tune,
What a liquid ditty floats
To the turtle-dove that listens, while she gloats
   On the moon!
Oh, from out the sounding cells,
What a gush of euphony voluminously wells!
   How it swells!
   How it dwells
On the Future! — how it tells
Of the rapture that impels
To the swinging and the ringing
Of the bells, bells, bells —
Of the bells, bells, bells, bells,
   Bells, bells, bells —
To the rhyming and the chiming of the bells!

Edgar Allan Poe

A good marriage is like a good handshake —
                    there is no upper hand.

Author Unknown

Long loved, long woo'd, and lately won,
My life's best hope, and now mine own.

Sir Walter Scott

To be loved is to know
happiness and contentment;
To give love is to know
the joy of sharing oneself.

Rebecca Thomas Shaw

JUNE WEDDING

The belief that June
is the happiest month for marriage
goes back to the days of Rome.
Juno — wife of Jupiter,
patroness of the young, and goddess of marriage —
is especially honored at this time.
The Romans felt that prosperity came to the man
and happiness to the maid married then.

THIS IS A HUSBAND

A husband is that special man
    You could write a book about,
The one you love to be with
    And couldn't do without.

A husband is a gentle look,
    A hand within your own;
He always makes you proud
    To feel that you are his alone.

A husband understands your moods
    And laughs at things you say;
He sees you at your worst
    And loves you anyway.

A husband is the one you kiss
    And make up with again
When there's a little difference
    Of opinion now and then.

He is that special man who shares
    All you're dreaming of
And gives a magic meaning
    To the wonder that is love.

Margaret Benton

THIS IS A WIFE

A wife is someone wonderful
    To come home to at night,
  Someone who shares your daily cares
    And makes the world seem bright.

A wife is understanding
    Of your changing moods and needs
  And looks for ways to please you
    With little, loving deeds.

A wife is a smile across the room,
    A gentle, warm embrace
  Whose tenderness and love for you
    Are mirrored in her face.

A wife is who you turn to
    When you need someone to cheer you;
  Your day is always happiest
    Whenever she is near you.

She's more than just a partner,
    She's the dearest thing in life,
  The girl who'll always make you proud
    To say, "This is my wife!"

Thomas Malloy

Life is a peaceful walk
        through quiet meadows,
    a song of joy,
        a sun-kissed morning,
    a star-swept sky,
        a new world dawning...
            when you're in love.

Marjorie Wright

RECIPE FOR A HAPPY MARRIAGE

Take a girl with starry eyes,
    Add a proud young man,
Blend with some exciting dreams —
    Perhaps a special plan —
Mix with two hearts filled with love
    That lasts "forever after,"
Season well with happiness,
    Companionship and laughter —
Put together in a home
    With a sunny atmosphere
And you'll have the kind of marriage
    That grows happier every year!

Elizabeth Gerus

BUTTERCUP FIELDS

I remember our first summer...
  Buttercup fields
  And the scent of hay.
I remember evening falling...
  And walking hand in hand
  At the close of day.
Sunsets seemed so much more lovely...
  Than sunsets
  Ever seemed before,
When you and I would walk together...
  In buttercup fields
  In the days of yore.
Somehow summer never left us...
  We saved its sunshine
  In our hearts,
And never knew the chill of winter...
  For we shared the warmth
  That love imparts.
Thanks for all the joys of summer...
  More than that
  What can I say?
Except that always I'll remember...
  Buttercup fields
  And the scent of hay.

Robert A. Wood

MARRIAGE IS MANY THINGS

Marriage is made of many things...
    it begins with vows
    and wedding rings...
       and love.
Marriage is a husband and wife
    who tenderly pledge
    to share one life...
       one love.
Marriage is dreams and sunshine bouquets,
    it's together times,
    joy-kissed days...
       and love.

Amanda Bradley

My heart to thy heart,
*   My hand to thine,*
My lips to thy lips,
*   Kisses are wine.*

Paul Laurence Dunbar

LOVE'S GARDEN

Marriage opens the gate
    to love's gentle garden;
Their promise made, the bride and groom
    rush in to greet life
      lying splendid before them.
Together they discover
    the rich perfume and melodious
      song of love;
They share nature's secrets,
    her happiness;
      and standing beneath a willow...
    they kiss.

Tina Hacker

WEDDING BLESSING

God bless your hearts
    That now are one,
God bless the life
    You've just begun,
God grant the things
    You're dreaming of —
A perfect marriage...
    A perfect love.

Barbara Burrow

I SAW TWO CLOUDS AT MORNING

I saw two clouds at morning,
   Tinged by the rising sun,
And in the dawn they floated on,
   And mingled into one:
      I thought that morning cloud was blest,
      It moved so sweetly to the west.

I saw two summer currents
   Flow smoothly to their meeting,
And join their course, with silent force,
   In peace each other greeting;
      Calm was their course through banks of green,
      While dimpling eddies played between.

Such be your gentle motion,
   Till life's last pulse shall beat;
Like summer's beam, and summer's stream,
   Float on, in joy, to meet
      A calmer sea, where storms shall cease,
      A purer sky, where all is peace.

John G. C. Brainard

Love is the smile
      on the face of the world.

Mary Dawson Hughes

LOVE

Love is a plant that, tended well, succeeds;
    Untended, it is starved and choked with weeds.
Love cultivated, roots, grows strong with living;
    And blossoms like the summer rose, with giving.

Emily Carey Alleman

Marriage . . .
*   Trust is the start of it,*
*   Joy is part of it,*
*   Love is the heart of it.*

Barbara Kunz Loots

LOVE UNITES YOU

Softly, softly,
    Love enfolds you,
Beckons, brightens,
    Strengthens, holds you...
Sweetly, sweetly,
    Love invites you;
Tenderly, tenderly,
    Love unites you!

Mary Dawson Hughes

SEASONS OF LOVE

Spring
> I love you in the springtime,
>> When the sky is clear and blue,
>
> And all the days are lovelier
>> Because they're spent with you.

Summer
> I love you in the summer,
>> Through each carefree, sunny day,
>
> With a love that goes much deeper
>> Than words could ever say.

Autumn
> I love you in the autumn,
>> When the leaves are red and gold,
>
> And we harvest all the happiness
>> Two loving hearts can hold.

Winter
> I love you in the wintertime,
>> When frost is in the air,
>
> And the world becomes a wonderland
>> Of happiness to share.

Rebecca Thomas Shaw

THE GIFTS OF MARRIAGE

These are the gifts of marriage —
    A home for you to share,
    A gentle hand for you to hold,
    A smile to ease your care.

These are the gifts of marriage —
    A faith that's ever true,
    A heart that's understanding
    And belongs alone to you.

These are the gifts of marriage —
    Blessings from up above,
    And the most important one of all
    Is the wonderful gift of love.

George D. Walley

THE TOUCH OF LOVE

Love puts the beauty
      in everyday things —
    the comfort in a touch,
    the music in a word,
    the warmth in a home,
    the joy in a memory,
    the "we" in a dream.

Karen Ravn

from THE COURTSHIP OF MILES STANDISH

Onward the bridal procession
　　now moved to their new habitation,
Happy husband and wife, and friends
　　conversing together.
Pleasantly murmured the brook,
　　as they crossed the ford in the forest,
Pleased with the image that passed,
　　like a dream of love, through its bosom,
Tremulous, floating in air,
　　o'er the depths of the azure abysses.
Down through the golden leaves
　　the sun was pouring his splendors,
Gleaming on purple grapes, that,
　　from branches above them suspended,
Mingled their odorous breath with the balm
　　of the pine and the fir-tree,
Wild and sweet as the clusters
　　that grew in the valley of Eshcol.
Like a picture it seemed of the primitive,
　　pastoral ages,
Fresh with the youth of the world,
　　and recalling Rebecca and Isaac,
Old and yet ever new,
　　and simple and beautiful always,
Love immortal and young
　　in the endless succession of lovers.
So through the Plymouth woods
　　passed onward the bridal procession.

Henry Wadsworth Longfellow

A HEART FILLED WITH LOVE

Love is a gift that cannot be demanded,
    A blessing that comes from the heart,
    And those who are sharing it
        find their thoughts turning
    To heaven, where love had its start.
Love is a pledge that will never be broken,
    A trust that will ever be true,
    And when it is sent from an unselfish heart,
    It's returned in full measure to you!

                Emily Ashley Tipton

MOST REMEMBERED

He told his love with orchids,
    With brooch of silver spun;
He bought her a gay parasol
    To twirl against the sun.

Then, in a summer meadow,
    With tender hands he wove
A necklace of white daisies,
    A token of true love.

Of orchids, brooch and parasol
    Faint memories now remain,
But etched for time upon her heart,
    A simple daisy chain.

                Katherine Edelman

A TOAST

Here's to the Bride!
    And here's to the Groom!
Here's to the beauty
    Of young love in bloom!

Here's to blue skies
And bright, sunny weather
Through the wonderful years
    Of a lifetime together!

Katherine Nelson Davis

WONDERSOME LOVE!

It's found 'twixt the twigs
    in the Munch-Apple tree,
'Tween tulips 'neath buddycups shy,
Tucked tiny in grasses
    by pebblefull brooks,
In fluffsome white clouds in the sky...
The buzzlebees sing it,
    the brisk breezes fling it
On flutterby wings high above;
It's sprinkled on everywhere,
    everyone knows,
It's wondersome, tenderful love!

Ellen Sloan

OUR WEDDING PRAYER

We stand before thine altar now
　　To pledge our lives, our hearts —
To make a sacred, holy vow
　　Now, as a new life starts.
And as we share one life, one name,
　　May we be ever true, .
Quick to praise and slow to blame,
　　Patient and helpful, too.
Grant that our home will always be
　　Thy home, year after year —
A haven of love and harmony
　　With Thy sweet presence near.
And give us, Lord, a portion of
　　Thy love that we might see
A glimpse, within our own true love,
　　Of immortality.

Barbara Burrow

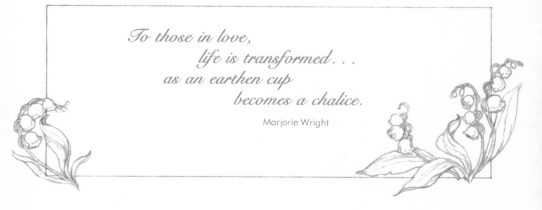

To those in love,
*　　life is transformed...*
as an earthen cup
*　　becomes a chalice.*

Marjorie Wright

THE BEST DAY TO WED

Wed on Monday, always poor,
    Wed on Tuesday, wed once more,
Wed on Wednesday, happy match,
    Wed on Thursday, splendid catch,
Wed on Friday, poorly mated,
    Wed on Saturday, better waited.

Monday for health,
    Tuesday for wealth,
    Wednesday the best day of all,
Thursday for losses,
    Friday for crosses,
    And Saturday no luck at all.

WEDDING BELLS

Wedding bells are ringing,
    Merry hearts are singing
    To the tune of perfect love.
    Hosts of friends are bringing
    Gifts to heighten future joy.

    Money cannot buy
    My wedding gift to you!
    'Tis made of love and friendship
    And wrapped in rainbow hue.

Emma F. Coffin

Marriage resembles a pair of shears,
     so joined that they cannot be separated;
often moving in opposite directions,
     yet always punishing anyone
          who comes between them.

Sydney Smith

HIAWATHA'S WEDDING FEAST

Sumptuous was the feast Nokomis
   Made at Hiawatha's wedding.
   All the bowls were made of bass-wood,
   White and polished very smoothly,
   All the spoons of horn of bison,
   Black and polished very smoothly,
      She had sent through all the village
   Messengers with wands of willow,
   As a sign of invitation,
   As a token of the feasting;
   And the wedding-guests assembled,
   Clad in all their richest raiment,
   Robes of fur and belts of wampum,
   Splendid with their paint and plumage,
   Beautiful with beads and tassels....

Henry Wadsworth Longfellow

YOU ARE PART OF ALL I LOVE

You are a part of all the things I love.
   I hear your happy voice when skylarks sing;
   I sense your touch in the fragile buds of spring;
   I see your eyes when bright stars shine above.
   When a gentle breeze moves through the grass
   And bends the leafy boughs as it weaves
   A silent pattern in the fields and trees —
   I see a gracefulness that only you surpass.
   I wonder, did I ever know the world
   Before our love began? This very hour
   I saw your beauty in a lovely flower
   With its sweet-scented petals still half-curled.
   In all the fair things that I adore,
   I see you, dear, and love you all the more.

George Webster Douglas

My bounty is as boundless as the sea,
      My love as deep; the more I give to thee,
   The more I have, for both are infinite.

William Shakespeare

WHEN TO MARRY

Marry when the year is new,
Always loving, kind and true.
  When February birds do mate,
  You may wed, nor dread the fate.
If you wed when March winds blow,
Joy and sorrow both you'll know.
  Marry in April when you can,
  Joy for maiden and for man.
Marry in the month of May,
You will surely rue the day.
  Marry when June roses blow,
  Over land and sea you'll go.
Those who in July do wed,
Must labor always for their bread.
  Whoever wed in August be
  Many a change are sure to see.
Marry in September's shrine,
Your living will be rich and fine.
  If in October you will marry,
  Love will come, but riches tarry.
If you wed in bleak November,
Only joy will come, remember.
  When December's snows fall fast,
  Marry and true love will last.

A HAPPY COUPLE

Happy —
   a bride in a white gown of lace,
Happy —
   a groom with a smile on his face,
Happy —
   these memories that time endears,
Happy —
   the joy that lasts through the years.

                              Ellen Green

THE LOVE KNOT

*Popular in the seventeenth century, the Knot of Love is
formed from interlacing loops which symbolize infinity
and signify a closely linked relationship. Written on the
entwining loops is the lover's poem, a poem which
forms a continuous message of love with neither beginning nor ending.*

This true love knot to thee, my dear, I send,
   An emblem of my love without an end,
A token of the gift I offer thee:
   Devotion that will last eternally.
Crossing, turning, winding inside out,
   Never ending, turning round about,
To symbolize the love so deep and true
   That I will feel forever, dear, for you.

                              R. W. Lawrence

55

To make a good husband, make a good wife.

John Heywood

THE WEDDING RING

The reasons given for the wearing of the ring upon the fourth finger of the left hand are three:

The most practical and mundane is the Roman explanation that this finger best protects the valuable ring. The left hand, to begin with, is used less than the right; therefore, the ring belongs to the left. And of the fingers on the left hand, the fourth is the only one which cannot easily be extended except in the company of another. The finger is protected: the ring is as safe as it can be.

The second reason goes back to the Egyptians, who believed that a vein ran from the fourth finger of the left hand directly to the heart. Since the heart controlled both life and love, this finger was the most honored. It deserved the ring, the pledge of love.

The third reason stems from the Christian Church which, to impress the seriousness of the ceremony upon the bride and groom, lectured that the thumb and first two fingers of the hand stood respectively for the Father, the Son, and the Holy Ghost, and that the fourth stood for the earthly love of man for woman, their marriage together, and the hope of Heaven to follow.

56

"With this ring I thee wed, and this gold and silver I thee give, and with my body I thee worship, and with all my worldly chatels I thee endow." When the groom had said these words, he held the ring for a moment over the tip of the thumb of the ring hand, saying, "In the name of the Father"; then held it briefly to the tip of the second finger, saying, "And of the Son"; then put it to the tip of the third finger, saying, "And of the Holy Ghost"; and, lastly placed it firmly on the fourth finger with a resolute "Amen."

There is nothing holier in this life of ours than the first consciousness of love, the first fluttering of its silken wings.

Henry Wadsworth Longfellow

And such a bliss is there betwixt them two
That, save the joy that lasteth evermo,
There is none like, that any creature
Hath seen or shall, while that the world may dure.

Geoffrey Chaucer

B lest is the bride on whom the sun doth shine.

Robert Herrick

BRIDAL COLORS

Married in blue, love ever true,
   Married in white, you've chosen right,
Married in red, you'll wish yourself dead,
   Married in black, you'll wish yourself back,
Married in gray, you'll go far away,
   Married in brown, you'll live out of town,
Married in green, ashamed to be seen,
   Married in pink, of you only he'll think,
Married in pearl, you'll live in a whirl,
   Married in yellow, jealous of your fellow.

F rom looks and smiles
    when our world was new,
From tender moments
    to love...
    we grew.

Mary Alice Loberg

SONNET 116

Let me not to the marriage of true minds
Admit impediments. Love is not love
Which alters when it alteration finds,
Or bends with the remover to remove:
O no; it is an ever-fixed mark,
That looks on tempests, and is never shaken;
It is the star to every wandering bark,
Whose worth's unknown, although his height be taken.
Love's not Time's fool, though rosy lips and cheeks
Within his bending sickle's compass come;
Love alters not with his brief hours and weeks,
But bears it out even to the edge of doom.
    If this be error, and upon me prov'd,
    I never writ, nor no man ever lov'd.

William Shakespeare

How sweet the mutual yoke of man and wife,
    When holy fires maintain love's heavenly life!

Richard Crashaw

WHAT IS A WEDDING?

A wedding's an altar
   With flowers — a prayer,
A blush and a smile
   And a hush in the air.
A wedding is Lohengrin
   Played sweet and low,
A ring, a bouquet
   And two faces aglow.
A wedding is vows
   From the heart, sweetly spoken —
A pledge of true love
   That's forever unbroken.
A wedding's the start
   Of a bright future life,
As two become one —
   Husband and wife.

Mary Ellen Lowe

Text set in Futura Light, a typeface designed by Paul Renner in 1927 for Bauer typefoundry.
Start letters set in Delphian Open Titling, created for Ludlow in 1928 by R. Hunter Middleton.
Printed on Hallmark Eggshell Book paper.
Designed by Leanne Mishler.